The Trading Floor

The T.R.A.D.I.N.G. Experience™
www.thejanetblair.com

PUBLISHED BY THOMAS PUBLISHING 2017

The Trading Floor

COMPLETE GUIDE ON HOW

FOREIGN EXCHANGE (FOREX) TRADING WORKS

Trading Strategies, Work from Home, Day Trading,
Double Your Income, Trading Platforms, FX, News

By Award Winning Author

Janet Blair

Thomas Publishing 2017

FOREWORD

The vast majority of traders are talking about the money you can make when the market drops. How trading can make you rich and how the stock market offers the best opportunities yet nobody talks about the price you are going to pay in the long run: unless you trade your old life for your dream life, now.

What happens when you shift your mindset from chasing opportunities into becoming the opportunity!

"Market trends,"
"Benchmark,"
"Charts,"
 "The power of brands,"
"Standard deviation,"
"FX traders,"

These are all words that can only become part of your vocabulary when you understand your worth. Can you afford not to take that journey?

Over time, Janet, the award-winning author of 'The Trading Floor,' helped traders not only to move commodities and currencies but to create their identity. Her latest book provides a new concept that will give you the tools you need to trade and the mindset to create the mental shift you need, to arrive where you belong.

In fact, when you attend Janet's workshop; The T.R.A.D.I.N.G Experience™ as a new student or an experienced FX trader, you will leave with a system that will never leave you. You will learn to monetise your existing abilities and also examine what makes you who you are. You will turn your life around and once you work with

Janet's unique system, the standards of your thinking will evolve and influence the standards of your life.

When most traders choose the currency game; many create their own rules and manage to control the benefits of the marketplace, gain unfair economic advantages and adopt strategic thinking.

Do you want to make uncapped progress within trading?

As you are reading this join the global community of movers and shakers that Janet is creating. Once you own your system, you can apply it day in, day out, for as long as you decide. You choose the timeframe, the market and the level of trading. Janet's system is designed for you to trade your old life for your dream life.

Marina Nani, Founder, Academy of Significance

ABOUT THE AUTHOR

I can remember when a special year of my life was coming up. I informed my husband at the time that we could not continue our relationship like this. I wanted change. It was around June of the following year when I decided there must be a better life than this. There had been no change and I had given him several warnings about our future. I tried everything possible to ensure we had a happy marriage.

There comes a point when enough is enough. You cannot change anyone who doesn't want to change themselves. I took my two children; left my husband and our beautiful three-bedroom home, to move in with my mum in her one bedroomed apartment. I remembered praying "God please help us!"

Society has us believe that because there is a divorce, your children will fail. My daughter was studying for her GCSE's at the time, she gained A's and B's in her exams in addition to winning a Youth BME education award (BME).

Also during this time, I had work issues. I had just completed my MBA and was moved to a secondment position with no option to return to my previous post. I applied for three other jobs, and was offered all three. I had no idea what was next for me and with no money I decided to take the temporary contract instead of the two permanent ones.

Many people would ask why I would want to give up the option of certainty for uncertainty. I trusted God. He had a plan for me.

Change of Direction

I received an email about trading which I was fascinated by. I have always been interested in finance so I opened a demo account and starting practicing. I accumulated a lot of money and lost it all. I believed that if I could make this money on a demo account, I should be able to do the same with a live account. My aim was to learn from experienced professionals so I decided to study with a reputable company based in London. My trading education cost me £20k but today this price has been reduced massively.

After working as a contractor for three years providing a consultancy service to the NHS they offered me a permanent role. Once again I turned it down. I saw trading as an opportunity that provided unlimited income. The corporate sector has a very good way of boxing us into a career path and putting a ceiling on how much we can earn. I knew this was not for me.

Unknown Opportunity

I started working with a trading company which gave me the skills and ability to teach; train, coach and mentor others in a trading floor experience. Then the company I was working for went into receivership. In 2012 an opportunity arose whereby the clients asked me to continue providing mentoring services to them and they would pay me directly. During this time my mother was very ill with dementia and kidney failure. This opportunity came at the right time to stay at home and start my trading business while looking after my mother.

Live the life you deserve

Working from home trading and providing mentoring to clients gave me freedom and flexibility. Sadly, my mum passed away in 2014 but I am truly grateful for her and how she raised me to be an independent woman.

I started my company called JPS Capital Trading in April 2012, providing trading training across the globe.

One of my clients entered a trade where she bought the USDJPY and gained 1,000 pips with my guidance. To put this into a monetary aspect, if you were trading £10 per PIP, this is equivalent to £10,000.

Another client, without any trading experience, traded commodities and made £26k. Join me on 'The T.r.a.d.i.n.g.' programme, www.thejanetblair.com or email me at janet@thejanetblair.com for further information.

If I can do it, you can too!
I will teach you how to trade smarter.

DEDICATION

I would like to give thanks to my creator Jesus who has given me the strength and confidence to face this world no matter what I am going through. "I can do all things through Christ which strengthens me" (Philippians 4:13).

Firstly, I would like to dedicate this book to my two children; Shanice McAnuff and Jermaine McAnuff. They have allowed me to travel the world without moaning about leaving them repetitively! Thank you both, for being understanding and supportive of having an entrepreneurial mother.

Secondly, I would also like to thank Christine Clayford for giving me access to her book writing programme and allowing me to research and follow each step.

Thirdly, a large thank you to Marina Nani for taking my book to the next level and for giving me the author's award. This has resulted in my book going viral and has sparked an interest in my trading programme. Thank you for highlighting that I have a system that will help both men, and women to understand what I do and how I can help them to exchange their old life for their dream life.

Thanks to my friends; Sonia Poleon, Serah Lister, Mike Douglas, Anthony Lyken, Darren Jones, Naomi Soako, Claudine Reid and Patrick Reid who believed that I had something to share that could encourage, change and transform people's lives.

CONTENTS

Foreword   2

About The Author   4

Dedication   7

Introduction   11

Trading   13

Relationships   26

Attitude   37

Destiny   42

Innovations   45

News   51

Growth   60

Bonus   65

Are You Ready to Gain More Knowledge?   70

Thank You   73

References   74

Glossary   76

"If you don't design your own life plan,
chances are, you'll fall into someone else's plan.
And guess what they have planned for you? Not much."
Jim Rohn

"Never depend on a single income.
Make investment to create a second source."
Warren Buffet

"Money was never a big motivation for me, except as a way to
keep score. The real excitement is playing the game."
Donald Trump

"If there is no price to be paid, it is also not of value."
Aphorism

"A man's worth is no greater than his ambitions."
Marcus Aurelius

INTRODUCTION

Over the last 20 years trading has moved into a different dimension. This kind of business was only available to institutions such as banks, hedge fund managers and excluded retail traders. Trading during the 1960's, the buying and selling of commodities, foreign exchange (FX) and other trading instruments were done mainly by paper. This in turn would then be delivered to a specific location to ensure the buy and sell orders were executed. Due to the technological evolution across the globe, it has allowed retail traders to trade anywhere in the world from their computers. The world has evolved.

The 21st century is affected by the technological change in every area of our lives and businesses. As the world has evolved, according to Doyle (2008), globalisation has caused many businesses to rethink the way they provide goods and services to their clients. According to Doyle (2008), because of competitors, the World Trade organisation (WTO) has been lowering barriers between countries to open up the market of such companies as Microsoft and McDonald's who are selling in the global markets. But it has proven difficult for smaller companies to utilise this strategy as they lack the economics of scales to remain competitive over the long run.

The world is in a digital age; many people now have a smartphone which has internet access or other online applications that will enable them to have many choices. Consumers are more interested in 'transactional convenience' than in location and accessibility.

Are you ready for trading?

Over the years, I have met several people who have told me that 'trading is not for me as I don't like mathematics or they have researched online and 'it is not for them.' What people fail to understand is there are many teachers, trainers, trading strategies and trading platforms that can be found on the internet. Individuals who want to become successful at trading need to spend time on focusing on one professional trainer's proven strategies on one particular platform.

All one needs is passion and a career that will give them the freedom and income to live the lifestyle they deserve. With trading, you can achieve exactly that. It's a career which is rewarding and fulfilling. Trading can give you the income, freedom and lifestyle that you want. It can also allow you to achieve the DREAMS you have always wanted. Under my guidance at www.thejanetblair.com, you will fulfil those dreams.

CHAPTER 1

TRADING

Walking you through the process of recreating your life from what you want to your ultimate success.

"Never, never, never give up."
Winston Churchill

What is trading?

We live in a world where there are always transactions taking place. The exchange of various goods or services is critical to everyone's daily life. A trade may be in the form of cash or kind. In the early centuries 6000 BC, trades used to exist between a buyer or a seller in exchange for something which was required by the next person. During the 1930's, this model was implemented during the great depression. Many used the bartering system in exchange of goods for services. Within some cultures this model still exists.

As the system starts to get complex, the world has moved on to producing money, whereby one can exchange cash for goods or services. While the use of cash is important there needs to be a buyer and seller. The same transaction takes place in the world of trading. During the next few chapters I will introduce you to the world of trading while going through what Forex (Fx), stocks, equities and the commodities market involve. I will introduce you to the correct terminology and show you how you can create an investment portfolio to build growth and wealth.

Trading will reduce your working hours and create passive income. This chapter will outline the reasons why you can become a trader and which market you can trade in. Also who trades the market and how you can make money similar to banks and fund managers. 'The Trading Floor' is a guide to illustrate how you can double your income and live the life you deserve.

Do any of the questions below speak to you?

- Do you want to make an extra income?
- Are you feeling tired of working a 9-5 without being paid what you are worth?
- Are you a single mother looking after your children?
- Are you a husband who wants to look after his family and plan for their future?
- Are you someone who deserves a good lifestyle?
- Do you want to start your own business working from home? If your answer is YES to any of the above questions, then read on... This book is for you.

Trading FX

There is no doubt that trading the markets is essential to achieving your dreams and gaining financial freedom. If you want to live the lifestyle you want and to leave a legacy for your family, there are several markets you can trade.

How is it possible to trade several markets?
When you consider the globe as a whole, there are many different countries and within each country they all have their own currency to exchange for goods or services. For example many countries may trade with the US Dollar; however each country has their local currency that they use. The UK currency is called the British Pound. Using different FX currencies provides the opportunity to trade anywhere in the world and at any time.

With my training programmes and strategies you will be able to trade all the markets using essential tools. These will ensure you have maximum profits and gain your life's fulfilment by using leverage.

Financial leverage

What is leverage?

Have you heard of the saying 'using other people's money'? This book will explain how you can do exactly that. It will enable you to make money online and/ build a profitable business. Trading the market is a bonus for both newbies and advanced traders. Outside of bankers, fund managers and other institutional traders are retail traders, just like you and I. Retailers do not have large capital or funds to deposit in their trading account. In my further chapters, I will explain the advantages and disadvantages of leverage.

Unlike the stock market, FX is one of the largest trading financial markets across the globe according to Investopedia (2015). It's a decentralised market whereby brokers (I will explain this term later) create price levels of currencies traded between the buyer and the seller.

Foreign Exchange Market (FX)

One would believe that FX is a physical market such as traded items like commodities. This market operates globally through computer group links with other banks and participants just like you and I.

What does the word 'Forex/FX' actually mean?

According to Investopedia, Forex (FX) is the market in which currencies are traded. It's the largest, most liquid market in the world with average traded values of $5 trillion dollars per day. All currencies around the world are traded in this market.

Too many newbies have heard how you can become rich trading in the FX market in next to no time. Or you may have heard that FX offers a 'get rich quick scheme' by marketing gurus who want to sell their courses. To others, it's a market that you will struggle with until you change your mindset and the way that you approach the market on a daily basis. Our state of mind has to be in tune with how the market operates.

Being an FX trader can be one of the most fulfilling and successful careers you will ever embark on. Having the skills and being able to master the art of trading is a huge benefit in allowing you to obtain financial freedom.

In the past stocks and FX used to be traded using manual/paper format. Over the years, we have moved on to become an e-commerce world. Therefore, currency trading is conducted electronically over-the-counter (OTC) by computers. This market is open 24 hours a day, trading five and a half days per week. International markets such as; London, New York, Tokyo, Zurich, Frankfurt and Hong Kong trade across almost every time zone.

Listed below are major currencies that trade across each country and are traded by banks, retailers and other market makers. The UK has the most traded currency in the world followed by the USA. When trading FX, there are very few regulations governing the cross-border trading of FX. However greater risks are involved in foreign trading. The fluctuating price of the dollar in any given country will increase the risk of losing money.

A recent regulation was passed in China to control the influx of FX and it was designed to balance the inflow and outflow of the market. Since 1995, China has fixed its exchange rate in order to create economic stability by fixing 8 Yuan to 1 US dollar. This has made it difficult for companies to compete in trade across the globe. According to the President of the United States Donald Trump; in April 2017, he will stop labelling China as a currency manipulator. China's goods and services remain cheap as they are one of the main manufacturers in the world.

One of the advantages of trading FX is that the market is open twenty-four hours a day. The market timings change from Asia to Europe and so on. Knowing this, allows the trader to buy and sell his/her assets at his/her complete advantage.

The trade of FX is affected by the fluctuation in exchange rate of currency of a particular region which is affected by the macro- economic conditions of a particular country. The trade deficits

GDPs (gross domestic product), inflation and budgets of a region are special indicators of the coming trend. These have to be followed if one wishes to take a sound investment and earn money.

Apart from the investment point of view, the moving of funds and currencies from one country to another, is also facilitated by the FX market. FX dealers across the globe earn huge sums of money while helping companies or individuals to transfer their funds from one country to another.

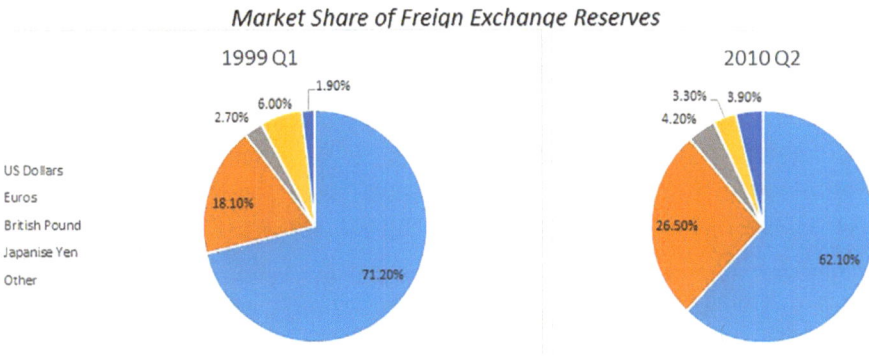

Figure 1 : Market share reserves

On a daily basis, traded transactions for each country and currency are listed (an example is below.) The US currency is the most traded currency in the world. Goods and services are an exchange in dollars instead of the local country currency (*see figure 2*).

Country	Daily Market Share (%)
Pound Sterling (GBP)	13
Euro (EUR)	39
Japanese Yen (JPY)	19
United States Dollar (USD)	85
Australia Dollar (AUD)	8

Figure 2 : Country currency utilisation

When you have decided to become a trader, these are the currencies you may want to focus on to become successful. There are other currencies you can trade; however, they may be costly in particular for a beginner trader. Especially one who does not have the capital to withstand the spread for other currencies (I will explain the term 'spread' later.)

Currencies that are not part of the major currency group are classed as 'exotic.' This simply means that not many traders will be trading these currencies and therefore, prices will remain static. Sometimes they can even remain the same all day because there are no buyers or sellers. Volume (total amount of currency traded daily) is also an important aspect to your trades as the market will move in price either going up or down and this is where you can make money. For example, when trading in the stock market if a particular stock has no buyers or sellers, the market price will be stationary sometimes all day or even several weeks. Also, if you buy stock and want to sell them and there are no sellers, this stock will be in your portfolio until someone wants to buy it from you.

It is important that you understand the risk of trading the markets and that you trade money you can afford to lose. Once you have completed my trading programme I will teach you how to trade the markets, minimising your risk and preserving your capital. The world's major currencies are in figure 3.

Major Currencies

Symbol	Country	Currency
USD	United States	Dollar
EUR	Euro Zone	Euro
JPY	Japan	Yen
CAD	Canada	Dollar
GBP	Great Britian	Pound
AUD	Australia	Dollar
CHF	Switzerland	Franc
NZD	New Zealand	Dollar

Figure 3: World's major currencies

Rank	Country/Organization	Gold holdings (in tonnes)	Gold's share of forex reserves
1	United States	8,133.5	71.6%
2	Germany	3,384.2	66.4%
3	International Monetary Fund	2,814.0	N.A.
4	Italy	2,451.8	65.8%
5	France	2,435.4	65.3%
6	Russia	1,206.8	12.0%
7	China	1,054.1	1.0%
8	Switzerland	1,040.0	7.5%
9	Japan	765.2	2.3%
10	Netherlands	612.5	53.9%
11	India	557.7	6.6%
12	Turkey	533.0	15.2%
13	European Central Bank	503.2	26.8%
14	Taiwan	423.6	3.8%
15	Portugal	382.5	78.1%
16	Venezuela	367.6	68.9%
17	Saudi Arabia	322.9	1.6%
18	United Kingdom	310.3	10.8%
19	Lebanon	286.8	21.2%
20	Spain	281.6	21.8%

Figure 4: Bloomberg (2015)

Many of us will travel to different parts of the world. But before travelling, you first need to know what the rate of exchange is. For example, when travelling to America from England, the exchange rate of the British Pound to the US dollar is 1.5155. Resulting in, any goods purchased in the United States have the conversion rate of; for every 1 USD spent, this is equivalent to 1.51 GBP.

The market is complicated with many strategies, algorithms, software and other trading tools available. Every trainer has their own system which they teach to their students.

Missed Opportunities

A trader does not have to make his or her life complicated. Life itself is complex enough. During my first FX training course I was taught to use indicators to become a profitable FX trader. I have been trading for over 11 years and I have found that indicators only obscure your vision. There are so many indicators that will obstruct your decision to trade, which will result in missed opportunities because the market is extremely fast paced. There is nothing more painful than a missed opportunity. I often explain to my students that there will always be opportunities but you have to develop the skills to learn how to identify them and then take ACTION!

I have met several people who insisted on learning to trade the markets by attending seminars, workshops, researching the internet and reading books. The aim in FX trading is to hone in on simple rules. One of the biggest challenges is to remain focused. If you can stay focused using one strategy at a time, you will become successful in the business of trading FX. You can get lost researching different methods online and trading strategies to trade. Simplicity is key. Look no further as my T.R.A.D.I.N.G.Programme™ will help you to take control.

A student of mine Philip Goodfellow, started trading over 20 years ago. He ran a successful business but decided to try trading as he wanted to spend more time with his family. After completing my training course, he is now making good money consistently through FX.

One of my rules is that if you want to learn anything in life, it's best to go and seek professional education or help. Many people do not want to pay for their education and do not see education as an investment. According to T. Harv Eker, creating a jar system will enable you to fund your education. He states that people should "stop waiting to manage your money..." You could research several years on the internet and end up losing a lot of money simply because you will be paying for your learning in another format. Rather than paying for it upfront so it's worth seeking help from a professional trader. Then, modeling what they do in less time in order to become successful.

To buy foreign goods or services as an investment from another country, companies or individuals first need to purchase the currency of the country that they are going to invest in. Here, the price of one currency is decided on the price of the other currency. This is called the 'exchange rate.'

The three prominent centres that deal with the bulk of the dealings are the United States, United Kingdom and Japan. The outstanding transactions are controlled from Australia, Germany, France, Switzerland, Singapore and Hong Kong.

Trading is done mostly in six major currency pairs, which are:

- EUR/USD
- USD/JPY
- USD/CHF
- AUD/USD
- GBP/USD
- USD/CAD

A trading day typically starts at 8am in London and concludes in Singapore and Hong Kong. When it is 1pm in London, the market in New York opens for business. Later in the afternoon, the San Francisco market opens and as this market closes for the day, the Singapore and Hong Kong markets start their day. Hence, trading goes on for 24 hours.

The currency trading is done via the internet and telephone. The online FX market is the newest phase of FX which allows even ordinary investors to have market returns. FX traders are also available to deal on behalf of ordinary investors.

As a trader, you should predict the behaviour of the other market partakers and this will enable you to beat competition by anticipating your opponent's strategies.

One way to evade unnecessary risk in FX is to avoid fraud dealers and those who are not regulated legally. Diversification is another way to manage risk. Trade on different currency pairs simultaneously to generate more entry level signals. Also, avoid high margin trades. You may also like to test your proficiency on the demo account provided for free.

The market is a merciless guerrilla and doesn't care if you are new to the industry or not. We have to come to the market with an edge. I don't mean to scare you but; be prepared to trade the markets, take all the knocks it gives you, review your trade and start a new day. Simply put, every day in trading is never the same.

Starting out as a new trader can be daunting especially when; you do not understand the terminology, trading platforms and who trades the market.

Capital preservation is one of the keys to trading. One of the biggest problems with new traders is they do not understand how to operate the trading platform, which will result in losing money faster than, if they had learnt how the trading platform worked in the first instance.

In this book, I will outline very simple trading strategies and techniques that I have used to make money while working as a project manager. With trading, you can create passive income that will allow you to spend time with your family or doing the things you love the most. Learning to trade shouldn't be sitting at a computer all day for 6 – 10 hours like working a 9-5 job.

Being a trader will give you the flexibility that you desire. In particular, stay at home mums/dads will benefit from being an FX trader. Simply because you can work from home or any location in the world as long as you have internet access. All you require is a laptop, computer, phone or tablet and a trading platform to perform your daily tasks (buy and sell currencies on the chart.)

Imagine being able to go bypass the stress of working 9-5, having no boss, no staff or commuting. Enjoying a stress-free life can be the most rewarding dream ever. All we need to do is focus on just trading the market and accepting what it has to offer us. PROFITS, PROFITS and MORE PROFITS!!!!

Making a living from trading

Let us take a look at the world of employment. Is there another way to make a living whilst reducing the time? Is it possible to have both? Most, if not all, economies require employees. The majority of the population of the world's economies are held in some form of employer to employee relationship. The employee does the work and the employer pays the wages or salary. The system works well, incredibly well for most of the time. It brings stresses and strains and these play themselves out in the lives of the individual employees. The employee is locked into a work situation that is dictated and controlled by others. They may gain limited freedom for some of the time but substantially, they are in harness and remain so until they are able to free themselves from the situation by finding alternative work or something else.

What is the 'something else?' The most obvious thing is to seek self-employment. Unfortunately, the odds of success outside of the often perceived safe and secure work environment are stacked quickly against them and they cannot find sufficient work to be able to survive. The road to success outside of employment is littered with individual and small business failure.

The pursuit of independence and autonomy continues. Within our human nature, we want to be FREE. Like a horse in harness, we are totally against being in a confined or constrained space. Our preference would be to become free which is all of our dreams. The question is, what can be done to change this problem and achieve our innermost desire to be free?

You could of course, be your own boss. Without question it is the most satisfying work one can carry out. How about finding a business that already provides an exit from employment and one that is already set up? All you have to do is learn how to operate it. Trading the FX market is as near to this as you can probably get.

You can start working in this new business for yourself immediately. You do not need permission or qualifications nor is there a need for big start- up capital. There is no need to carry out stock or inventory and you do not need employees or even customers.

All that is necessary is a little education and know-how, teamed with minimal capital to kick start your career in the FX market. My training programmes teach you to preserve your capital and ensure you manage your emotions whilst trading. Everything in this book are lessons I have learned over the past 11 years of my trading journey.

To trade in the FX market, there are only two outcomes. One - You win. Two - You Lose. Before you come to the market ensure you know where you will buy and sell. For example, if you plan your trades overnight and want to trade the UK session then you will need to review the current price in relation to your trade plan.

I often hear traders say "I think the market is going up so I will buy," or "I believe the market is going down so I need to sell." Never trade on what you 'think' or 'believe.' The market is unpredictable and the only indication on market trends is illustrated on the charts. The other kind of trader, is the procrastinator, the one who talks themselves out of a good opportunity. If you are to come to the market with this mindset, then trading is not for you. The market waits for no one and therefore it will leave you behind.

Trading terminology

Don't be put off with the terminology used in trading. Like any business, when you decided to take on a new career, job or industry, you will have to learn the terminology used and the same goes for the trading industry. These terminologies are simple when you get a hang of them, and you will learn these during my trading programme. You may also come across them sometimes on the news or TV.

Too many beginners in the market have heard of how they can become rich by trading the market in little or no time or with limited effort. Making money trading the markets will require very simple rules and terminology, which will become second nature.

Learning a different language can be daunting but once you have become a part of that community, speaking the language gets easier and easier and this is similar to trading.

When you go on holiday to another country, you have to exchange your money to the country's currency that you will be travelling to. For example, if you were travelling to America, (currently, as I am writing this, the exchange rate for the US Dollar to the British Pound is 1.29.) Therefore, if I am purchasing goods from the United States, then I will need to exchange my GBP to the USD: £1 = $1.29. (*see chapter 3*) These are common terminologies used in FX. Explanations for these have been simplified to make sense to the beginner and advanced trader. This can be found in the glossary at the back of this book.

CHAPTER 2

RELATIONSHIPS

Family. Your business. Your passion.

"People will forget what you said, people will forget what you did,
but people will never forget how you made them feel."
Maya Angelou

Relationships and the market

One of the attributes to creating a strong foundation of a successful business is developing a strong rapport with your customers. Tony Robbins' quote 'influence people' to get anything you want; is a mentality everyone should adopt when wanting to create any successful business. Most network marketers become millionaires by building a strong relationship with customers and getting the right team in place to encourage growth. You may question what does a relationship have to do with the FX markets? A strong relationship and understanding of the market will allow you to know; what drives the market, who trades the market and how to make a profit. Grasping this is paramount to creating a strong foundation to build a successful trading business. If you want to become a successful trader, you have to understand the 'herd' mentality.

The herd mentality

Not being influenced by the noise in the market will keep you away from executing trades based on emotions or adopting the behaviours of others. The markets have several facets, however, creating a simply strategy will help you weed out distractions.

How to implement a simple strategy?

Before you decide to start trading and building your business it is necessary to find out your character.

There is a saying: 'how you do anything is how you do everything." *T. Harv Eker.*

We can have so many trading strategies but it's how you apply this to your trading style. For a strategy to fully be applied and be successful, you have to create a daily programme by taking the trade at least 20 times. When we consider probability you could roll a dice six times, eventually the dice would show you the result you predicted, eventually you will win. This same principle applies to trading.

As we do not have any control over the market, it has a way of surprising us, if we are not prepared or in the right frame of mind. Whether you are a beginner or have been trading for years, no one can predict the market. There is always a winner and loser in every trading transaction. You are trading against another trader albeit financial institutions or a retail trader who wants to win. Statistics say that 95% of traders lose money. Let us examine this statement. If 95% of traders lose money, why do so many people want to learn how to trade? Having spent over 11 years trading, I have concluded a list of reasons why, 95% of traders lose money:

- No strategy or rules when trading the markets
- No mentor
- No professional training
- No appropriate risk management in place
- No understanding of the trading platform
- Lack of emotional control

The majority of the 95% of traders who lose money would have taught themselves how to trade online as they do not want to spend money learning. Throughout this book, I will address the need to pursue the right trading course. Having a simple strategy will equate to high probability and set up trades to maintain a winning system.

Creating a winning system has several facets. Trading is a business of risk, and won't guarantee profits every time you trade.

On the 20th October 2016, the news reporters revealed that the Euro was bearish (trading to the downside). Traders were already short or started to sell the Euro as they were convinced the base rate would be cut. Base rates are usually controlled by central banks across the globe. The base rate or interest rate is a percentage charge for lending to other banks and used as a benchmark for lending to retailers in particular mortgages and savings. In view of this, the market makers expected the European Central Bank (ECB) Minimum Base rate to be cut by .25 (*Figure 5*). This was expected, and traders were happy about the news of the minimum base rate cut by a quarter percent (¼ %). With this predicted, news which is explained as good news (I will explain in chapter six); results in the market reacted positively. In this instant, we saw the Euro spiking (trading higher) to the upside. The aim of this cut by the ECB was to expand its money printing programme and to stimulate economic growth. Sharply after the minimum bid rate cut, there was an ECB press conference where Mario Draghi, President of the ECB Central Bank spoke. As I mentioned in my previous chapters, your account could be in profit from a trade you took short (sell) before any news events and then suddenly the market changes direction to the upside. The market was expecting him to buy more bonds. However, this didn't happen, neither did he mention he was going to buy any. Shortly after based on this information, the market sold off to over 1.05% on the EUR/USD, after a strong move to the upside thus illustrating the market had no control and was/is unpredictable.

Having taken this trade, you would end up with a loss to the upside as you would be stopped out. If you didn't reverse the trade based on your rules or strategy, you would end up making a loss when you have taken over 50 – 100 pips from this trade.

Figure 5: Eurusd news trade

Simple Strategy

One of the trading strategies I would like you to learn will allow you to identify major levels on the chart with a simple horizontal line. Keeping these lines on your charting platform will allow you to identify trading entry levels as the price approaches a particular level as seen above (*figure 5*). Having strategies removes the emotion out of trading, teaching you to become a disciplined trader.

Calculating profits and losses

The impact on your capital will affect your trading psychology. Not knowing how to calculate your profit and losses is a risk of ruining your trading capital. One of my main aims is to teach new, intermediate and advanced traders how to calculate profit and loss. When learning how to trade, most people embark on a two or three-day course where they learn the fundamentals on how to trade. Then after the course is finished the learner is left to work out the market by themselves, due to high costs for mentors. My training programme includes access to me as a mentor and trainer for a very discounted rate.

The trade below in Figure 6, New Zealand Dollar and the United States Dollar NZD/USD, entry level sell below 0.6834. The market sold off to 0.6766 gaining a profit of 68 pips.

Figure 6: NZDUSD sell (short) trade with profits

To build a successful business one should have a strong foundation. I have outlined below how to calculate your profits and losses. You don't need to have a degree to be able to undertake simple calculations.

Profit

A trader is most joyful when he/she is making money daily. Let's be realistic; you are not guaranteed to make profits every single day. There are days when the markets will be in your favour, and other days you will suffer losses.

In order for your strategy to be simple, it starts by having an aim of how much money you want to make whether that be as a percentage or a monetary value. Your phone calculator is sufficient enough to work out your profits on. Whether you are a short term, long term or swing trader, you should always identify where you will take profit (take money from the market).

Calculating the pip value will determine your trading account profit on a particular currency pair you buy or sell (long or short). a trader can make money in the market when it is going up or down, compared to an investor.

An example can be seen in trading the GBP/USD (Great British Pound against the United States Dollar). The current price is 1.2885 (*13th May 2017*). Your planned profit is £200 meaning you want to take 20 pips (£10 per pips x 20 = £200) profit from the market. Once the price reaches your set profit target on your trading platform, it is time to sell.

Traders go wrong when they allow emotions to get the better of them. Some traders in this situation would have the profit target set at 20 pips profit and then once they achieve this, they will become greedy allowing the trade to continue opening their trade to risk of loss.

You can work out your daily profit target by using a basic spread-sheet, which I have given in my bonus chapter to help you stay on track and increase your capital.

Once you have the horizontal lines on your chart, this will prevent missed opportunities. The chart below shows the DOW trading above the 20,000 level trading to the upside. The example below shows how you can make money when the market goes up. A market can increase like this over days/weeks, which has resulted in the term "making money while you sleep" as the market and trades you have placed, are active even when you are not. One of the trading strategies I teach my students is to remove emotions from trading using the 'Set and Forget Strategy' (*Figure 7*).

Figure 7: DOW above 20000 level

You can make money when the market trades down (also referred to as 'short sell'), the example shown below illustrates this perfectly (*Figure 8*). As the market price moves below your sell entry level to the downside, from 82.12 to 81.51 with a stop loss at 82.230, you would have gained 61 pips. With 61 pips gained, provided you are trading at £10 per pip, this would equate to £610 in your trading account once you have closed the trade.

Losses

Making money trading is a great feeling, but when you are losing, it can be emotionally exhausting. It's about controlling your emotions when losses occur. during losses it might be difficult to manage your emotions. A trader ought to maintain similar emotions for winning

Figure 8: CADJPY make money short market

and losing. It is a good idea to start by knowing your account capital and then work out what you can afford to lose per day and per trade.

According to Ritholtz (2009), if you have a vigorous respect for losses and manage this on a daily basis, you will preserve your capital. Many traders who haven't had any trading education will look at trading like spinning the roulette wheel and hoping that their trades will be winners all the time. I am afraid this is not the case in the real world. As I mentioned when explaining profits, the same rules/principles apply to losses.

Before you take a trade, you should know exactly how much risk or loss you can withstand based on your trading capital. Also, you need to identify on the major chart levels where price may stop so you can protect your capital.

If you decide to buy the AUD/CAD at 1.02746, you should calculate the last swing low on the chart based on your trading timeframe. For example, if you are trading on a 30 minute, one hour, four hour or daily chart time frame, then your stop loss should be calculated below this level (*Figure 9*). If for example, you have decided to buy the AUD/CAD above 1.02746, your stop loss should be below this level based on the last swing high or low. If your swing low is 10 pips, which is a low-risk trade, then your losses should be based on your pip value, depending on your capital. Your pip value should always be taken into consideration. If I have £2,000 in my account, then my risk should be 1-2% of my capital.

Figure 9: AUDCAD buy (long, bullish) market

Market Condition

The market travels in three directions; up, down and sideways, which are shown across. Learning how to identify market directions will allow you to use the correct trading strategy as per market conditions to make profits.

Figure 10: Bull Market UP

Up Trend (BULL)

Figure 11: Bear Market DOWN

Downtrend (BULL)

Sideways (CONSOLIDATION)

Figure 12: Consolidated (sideways) Market

CHAPTER 3

ATTITUDE

Leading everyone as you create the team and the environment to answer the needs of the people first.

"Attitude is a little thing that makes a big difference."
Winston Churchill

The Mind Merger - Psychology

Over the past 11 years that I have been trading I have learnt first-hand that controlling your emotions and mental state is something that is paramount to your success as a trader.

Trading is one of the greatest teachers you will ever have in showing you your character and personality traits. I have asked many of my past students before they start trading: "what is your risk tolerance?" Many would respond "high."

However, when it comes down to having their real money on the line, many panic and this illustrates their risk levels actually being very low. Having the right attitude towards risk is one of the key elements in trading.

An example would be, if you and your friend were placing a bet on a horse to win a race. Sadly, the horse loses, meaning you will have lost your first bet. As human beings, we want to win all the time and not calculating your risk for the day means that you will place another bet with the aim to win again as this also ends in a loss. Some traders would continue not knowing when to call it a day.

Some people make a trade either buying or selling, without calculating the risk and when the trade starts going against their predictions they then realise that they stand to lose too much money and they exit out of the trade prematurely.

Many people will also increase their gain as they want to make more money than they will lose. In trading, the asymmetry is called 'loss aversion' which is often referred to as 'risk aversion' (Sharpe 2012).

Emotional checklist

When we enter the market to trade, we are aiming to grow our trading account (capital) and therefore aim to minimise any potential losses. Banks and institutional floor traders will often use robots to manage some of the trading emotions. Our emotions will sometimes cause us to procrastinate or prevent us from getting into a trade based on previous experiences especially if we have suffered significant losses in the past.

Managing our inherent emotional biases will help us to be at peace with our trading outcomes whether losses or gains. Emotional biases can result in us behaving irrationally and jumping into the markets without any thought or acting out 'revenge trading' (trading to retrieve any losses).

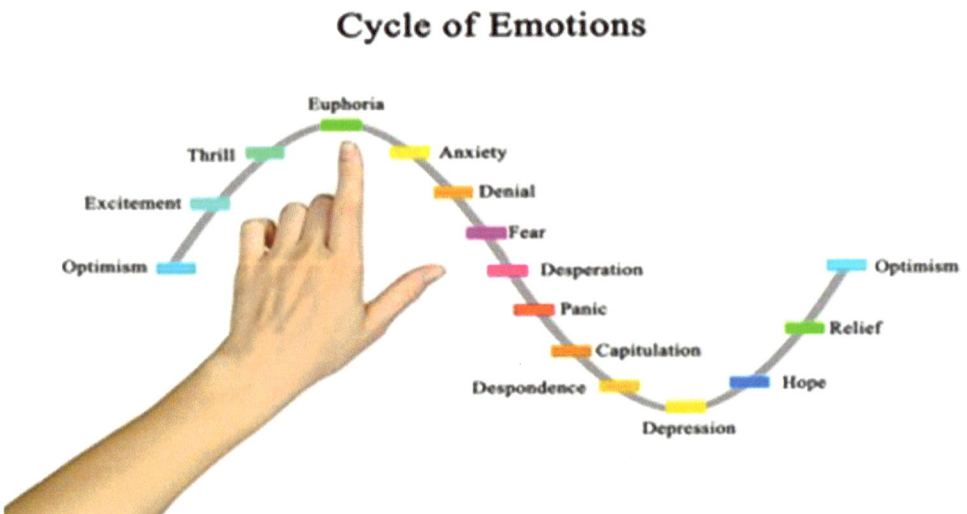

Figure 13: Cycle of emotions

Understanding the 14 stages of your emotional cycle can help to keep one calm in order to enjoying trading for a living.

Optimism – Planned our entry to buy or sell and feel about the trade.

Excitement – Moving from our entry level, we start to develop thoughts in our head of a winning outcome and what we could do with the money.

Thrill – Now we are over the moon as the trade is still going in our favour.

Euphoria – You have now reached a pinnacle. The outcome expected is more than what you anticipated. Not managing our risk.

Anxiety – So the price is now going below the highest point. Now we are thinking this trade will trade higher.

Denial – A feeling of misbelief as our feelings suggest the trade will get back to the price level it did before.

Fear - suffering losses may have an impact on our emotional state, therefore the fear of loss having a big impact on the way we trade.

Desperation – As we are trying to recover losses, we may not analyse the market before pressing the buy or sell button.

Panic – No idea as to which trade or what else to do to recover our losses.

Capitulation – To avoid further losses, we will exit the trade prematurely, although we quantify our risk/reward ratio.

Despondency – A particular currency part may cause us not to look at another profitable opportunity with a particular currency pair due to psychological damage.

Depression – Trying to justify within ourselves that it was the wrong reason to enter a trade. Feeling sorry about the missed opportunity.

Hope – Now we are feeling a great sigh of relief as price is trending up or down at the level we originally predicted.

Relief – Our faith in the market has now improved and we want to continue to trade after a profitable trade.

As part of the decision-making process of analysing and planning whether to buy or sell, each trader will go through this cycle. Having a clear understanding of how a $5 trillion-dollar market operates and bearing in mind that we have no control over it, will help our decision in trading. In view of this wealth of understanding, we will have a much better idea of how to operate to become a successful and profitable trader.

State of Mind

I know from time to time things may not be correct in our lives and this can affect our mental and physical state/or wellbeing. During my time at Durham College in Jamaica where I studied Business Studies, I have realised that worry can make you ill. Have you ever wondered why so many people are ill in this world? It's not because of the lack of money they have but often it is due to worry.

Overconfidence can become the number one killer in many people's trade. One of my clients had £5,000 in his trading account and decided to increase his pip value from £1 per pip to £10 per pip as he made money doing so with one or two trades previously. Overconfidence in his trades eventually ruined his capital and depleted his confidence in trading.

Even when performing your daily tasks, if you are not in the right state of mind, this can affect your performance. During my programme, clients are taught how to create an effective state of mind to trade the markets. To ensure you have the optimum performance, you have to enter the market knowing there are only two possible outcomes. Once someone has accepted any decision made whilst trading either results in a loss or a win, this makes trading very simple and easier to manage psychologically.

Rule Base Strategy

Having a trading plan is important. Creating a strategy that will work with your trading plan depending on market conditions will enable you to trade the FX market without losing too much of your initial capital.

Creating a trading strategy is very simple as mentioned in the previous chapter. Every country has rules and rules differ depending on where you are in the world. For example, public affection isn't acceptable in Middle Eastern countries such as Dubai. However Western countries such as the UK accept it. Like countries having different rules to function accordingly, industries also have to have different rules. FX trainers teach their own rules to their students to ensure a particular way of trading, this is called a Rule Base Strategy.

Do you want to become an intelligent trader?

To become an intelligent trader doesn't require a PHD, Masters, degree or a high IQ. Having these qualifications will bear no relevance to becoming an intelligent trader. You don't need to be a mathematician to trade successfully. The simple principles are discipline, patience, risk management and being able to control your emotions during trading. Also, to think quickly if a trade hasn't gone according to plan.

CHAPTER 4

DESTINY

Fresh perspective of the mind, to generate a new status in society for entrepreneurs.

"It is not in the stars to hold our destiny but in ourselves."
William Shakespeare

As a teenager I constantly achieved A's and B's in my science subjects. When it was time to choose my career path, I chose to be a secretary. My teacher Mr. Grant, enquired why I would choose a job not suited to my grades. He wanted me to progress onto being a doctor, scientist or lawyer, as he thought I was more than capable of an academic profession. But I was more than happy to leave school to be a secretary. Mr. Grant saw something in me all those years ago, something

I didn't even know was there. I am now so much more than a secretary. Currently, I teach people how to generate wealth on the FX and stock market which has transformed many of my clients' lives.

Ask yourself this question: Am I living a fulfilled life?

With my programme, I use the SMART goal setting formula:

S – specific (or important)
M – Measurable (or expressive)
A – attainable (or action-oriented)
R– relevant (or gratifying)
T- Time-bound (or Trajectory)

I would encourage you to do a 90-day plan for your trading career, using the SMART goal setting formula.

> "Time can be an ally or an enemy. What it becomes, depends entirely on you, your goals, and your determination to use every available minute."
> *Zig Ziglar*

After mapping out your plan; I have listed 5 steps below to help manage your account and to build your portfolio of asset diversification.

5 Steps to Grow Your Account

1. Define which markets you want to trade
2. List your criteria for trading these markets
3. Identify the trading strategy you are going to use for trading
4. Decide whether you will focus on; short, medium or long-term trading
5. Review financial outcomes from the trading strategy you have chosen

Portfolio builing
FX Market

As FX is one of the largest traded financial markets in the world, according to Investopedia (2015) there is no centralised marketplace. Therefore, currency trading is conducted electronically over-the-counter (OTC) by computers. The FX market is open for 24 hours a day, it trades five and a half days per week in international markets.

One can just focus on the FX stock market indexes to trade and make money as you are not buying individual stocks. For example, The S&P500 has 500 companies so you won't be buying or selling individual stocks. By trading this market, you can reduce transaction costs (brokerage fees) by taking advantage of the economics of scales (a group of companies rather than an individual company.)

Key Indices	Market	Current Level	Current PE
Dow Jones Industrial	USA	13,610.15	13.36
S&P500	USA	1,460.93	14.83
NASDAQ	USA	3,136.19	17.41
RUSSELL 2000	USA	842.86	34.79
FTSE 100	UK	5,871.02	13.22
DAX	Germany	7,397.87	14.19
CAC 40	France	3,457.04	12.08
KLCI	Malaysia	1,657.27	15.42
STI	Singapore	3,086.69	12.41
ASX 200	Australia	4,481.90	16.95
Hang Seng	Hong Kong	20,888.90	10.55
CSI 300	China	2,275.37	11.36
JCI	Indonesia	4,314.04	19.29
SET	Thailand	1,308.69	18.52
KOPSI	South Korea	1,983.03	17.07
NIKKEI 225	Japan	8,863.30	21.8

Figure 14: Bloomberg 2012 Foreign stock market indexes

CHAPTER 5

INNOVATIONS

"The secret of getting ahead is getting started."
Mark Twain

"If you want something new,
you have to stop doing something old."
Peter F. Drucker

The digital age has advanced the trading industry massively. Back in the 1970's trades were done manually by phone, via a broker or telex and therefore it would take some time for a transaction between the buyer and the seller to happen.

Brokers

There are several types of brokers who act as the middleman between the market and yourself. You can conduct your trade by contacting your broker on the telephone instructing him/her what to buy or sell based on the capital in your trading account. A broker can place your order based on three principal transactions; market order, limit order or short sells. As the market has evolved, you now have the option to do the same transaction yourself based on opening a brokerage account and funding your account with your personal money. You can execute your primary transaction simply by the touch of a button as long as you have internet connection.

With the improvement in communication and trade technology this has given rise to a constant price for trading different currencies across the financial centres of the world. Within this era a transaction can happen in a split second. The transaction (buying or selling) between the buyer and seller with innovations and technological change has to happen for many traders quickly without any hiccups. For example, once you place your trade to either buy or sell, if you do not have good internet connection, this could stop you from entering a trade or getting out of a trade due to poor connectivity. As a trader, it is advisable to have good internet connections or have your broker's telephone number to hand.

Pros and cons of FX mobile trading

Think about it. You can now use a mobile phone to trade FX anytime or anywhere. At home, work, on the train, in a restaurant, the possibilities are endless. With the latest generation of smartphones, you have a raft of tools for technical analysis, market information from brokers, and access to your trading account: all from one small device that fits neatly into your pocket.

Why would you ever go back to a PC for trading? Actually, for a number of reasons. As powerful as smartphones have now become, they can't do everything you can do on a PC. Take a look at some of the pros and cons of mobile FX trading below.

Advantages of FX mobile trading
Availability

Anywhere you can get a network connection for your mobile; you can trade FX. You no longer have to be glued to your PC. You don't even have to go searching for an internet cafe. Open one trading position in an elevator, close another one in a taxi, and open a third one in a bar and so on.

Existing accounts

The chances are that the trading platform you are operating with on the PC has an app for your mobile phone, allowing you to trade on the go. More than 500 FX brokers support access from mobile devices.

Train trading skills

Tired of playing "Angry Birds" on your mobile? Open a demo account and train your trading skills (analysing the market using technical indicators.)

Market analysis

Trading platforms available for mobiles often offer a wide variety of tools and indicators (30 or more) to let you analyse and predict what the market is going to do. The screen on your smart phone is smaller than the one on your PC, but it still has excellent resolution for zooming in and out. It also contains tons of colours for picking out your favourite chart patterns.

Mobility

It's not called a mobile for no reason. Not to mention the fact that the mobile beats the PC/laptop in reference to its compactness and lightness without a doubt.

Disadvantages of FX mobile trading

Dropped connections- sometimes (like in the elevator/in a basement) your mobile loses its internet connection. If you're in the middle of a critical trading manoeuvre, this can be intensely frustrating, and result in a potential loss of profit.

Mediocre execution time

Platforms for mobile access are often generated from platforms written for PCs. You might get the functionality, but you don't always get comparable performance, especially if the platform developers have not properly optimised their software for use with mobile phones. Likewise, PCs still have the edge overall when it comes to convenience in opening a trade. With a mobile, you may have to practice patience.

Additional costs

Depending on the phone plan you've chosen, and the type of internet access that is available, you may find connection costs running up to more than you imagined.

Lack of EAs

Those Expert Advisors, or similar trading automation tools, that you can use from your PC may simply not be available on your mobile. Your trading will therefore have to be manual, without the extended "set it and forget it" possibilities that you can have on your PC.

It's clear that these disadvantages have not deterred a considerable number of traders from adopting the mobile platforms for trading FX. After all you can still do a lot with the functions of opening and closing trades, and setting stop, loss and profit targets for orders from your phone.

Where does all that leave us with FX trading on mobile phones? In my opinion, the trading software for mobile phones still needs to improve its stability and functionality to catch up with trading platforms available for PCs. However, I do believe mobile devices can be convenient for analysing the market and practicing on demo accounts. I think you have to wait a little before scrapping your PC in favour of trading purely by mobile.

The mobile trend is fast growing, and more people have acquired mobile phones in recent times. With the advances in technology more consumers use their mobile phones for just about anything such as paying bills, shopping, searching for lower prices, online banking and many more. Given this, many traders use their phones to place, buy and sell orders including stop loss. There are applications where you can check your trades if you are busy. Keynote (2013), reported that in the UK, 78.1 million mobile handset connections and a further 4.9 million subscribe to mobile broadband; as smartphone ownership is on the rise, mobile usage has grown considerably. The brokers have developed their trading platform to accommodate traders so they have the functionality to trade anytime of the day using their smartphone or iPad. If you work 9-5, this is a great tool to be able to access your trades on your phone.

The FX market is worth over 5 trillion dollars. It is one of the most liquid markets that is traded by brokers, fund managers, banks, and in more recent times, retailers. A "retailer" can be a normal person who does not work in the bank. As retailers have access to this market, they can be trained to make money on the FX market which was exclusive to brokers, fund managers and banks in previous times. As mobile technology evolves to the next era, brokers have to keep up to speed with the different types of technological changes. retail traders have choices, and can compare which broker provides the best spread, and whether their trading platform can be accessed by the type of phone they have.

Forex Trading Leverage

Many start-ups require you to have a huge amount of capital before you can open a business. The interesting thing with trading is that you can borrow the brokers' money to trade with, which allows you a margin. Some brokers' trading platforms will allow you to trade with 50:1 (meaning the brokers' trading platform will multiply your initial capital by 50.) i.e. if you start with £1,000 this will allow you have £50,000 in your trading fund. (Disclaimer: Please note you can lose your initial capital plus more, meaning you can be in debt to the broker.) Although these brokers are offering that amount of money in your trading fund, you don't want to overexpose your account believing you have loads of money to trade. I would encourage you to start with £1,000 (10:1) the equivalent of £10,000 as a starting capital. This is called leverage.

Alternative Markets for Long-Term Investors

Once you've become an FX trader, you may want to look at long term investments and other markets as you develop your trading skills. Being a long-term trader, requires extreme patience and good psychological skills. There are other markets you can trade such as commodities, stocks and equities. In this chapter, I will explain the difference between commodities and FX markets.

Commodities vs FX markets

Trading on the FX is fast paced gaining results and/losses quickly, making this the perfect marketplace for day traders. These are referred to as 'same day/intra-day trades'. Gold and crude oil could also be put into that category.

If a trader is looking for a longer-term investment, trading commodities such as sugar, wheat and/corn are more appropriate for their requirements. These types of investments are called swing/long-term trades, lasting two or more days and even as long as several months or years.

CHAPTER 6

NEWS

"Buy the rumour and sell the facts"
Finance & Investment

Over the years, the media has created a fear amongst us all that trading the stock market is very risky and we could lose all our money. So why is it that we still leave our money in the hands of the banks who do exactly this with our money? Have you ever wondered why interest rates are only 1-2% EAR for the year? The reason why is simply because the banks want to keep as much profit as possible from investing our money on the stock market.

With my trading programme I will show you how you can take advantage of the market and trade your money yourself to gain more in percentage than what the bank offers (*Figure 15.*)

Double $5,772 in 1 month!!!!

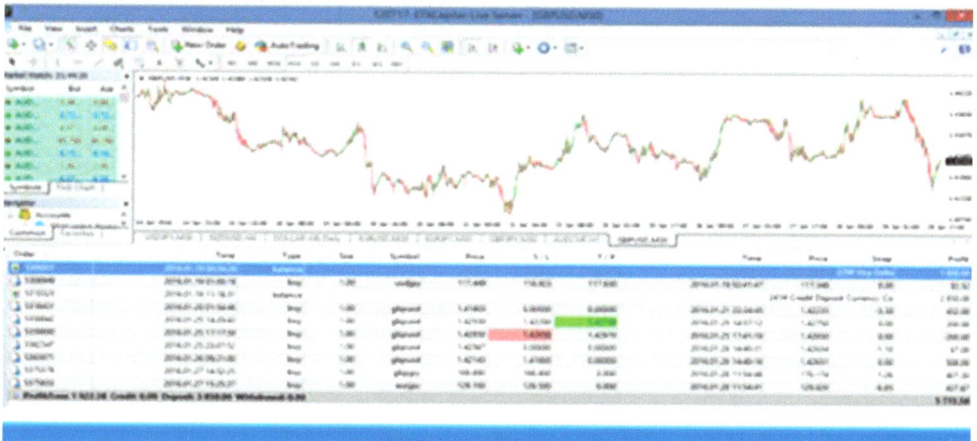

Brexit Referendum

On the 23rd of June 2016, a referendum was held for UK citizens to cast their votes on whether to remain in the European Union (EU). The EU is a partnership with 28 European countries based on economics and politics. This was agreed after World War 2 to build a stronger economy and trade relationship. Overall, 30 million people voted, giving a preference to leave the EU by 51.9% to 48.1%. Just before the announcement, the Pound grew stronger. However, once the results came out that "leave" won the vote, the British Pound fell more than 1,700 pips in price from the weekly high of 1.50116 to 1.32190 (*Figure 16.*) As I mentioned in previous chapters, using horizontal lines as a trading strategy, takes out the emotions as you will be in the market at the right time, once the British Pound traded to the downside.

Figure 16: GBPUSD Weekly

Election Trading Predictions

Over the years 2014 – 2017, there have been several elections for presidency such as in; United States, Netherlands, South Africa, France and United Kingdom. Trading around an election brings several opportunities to make/lose money quickly. Analysing and planning your trade in advance is vital to your trading success. Using my simple horizontal lines strategy, you can make money when the market goes up or down (*Figure 17*).

Figure 17: After Brexit British Pound 1.19085

In view of the UK election, the British Pound is now trading at 1.2910 level, halfway to the price it was almost a year ago 1.50197. Despite all the negative news and press about BREXIT, the British Pound remains strong. As a technical analyst, 'trade what you see' with a view to understand the macroeconomic to make a trading decision. Since the US presidential election in November 2016, where Donald Trump came into power, during his first 100 days, we have seen the stock market such as the DOW, S&P and NASDAQ gain over 200 points and continue to trend to the upside (*Figure 18*).

What is a Fusion Analyst?

To become a fusion analyst trader, one has to combine technical and fundamental trading.

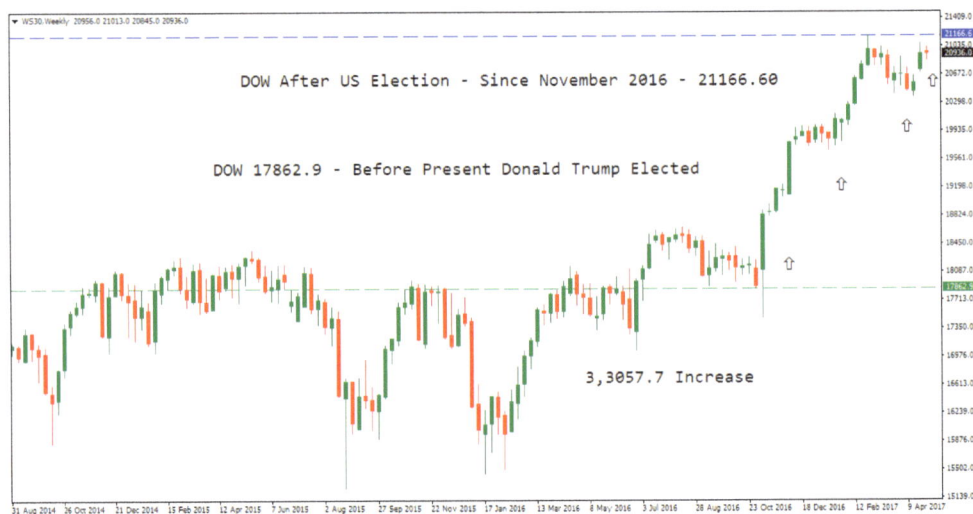

Figure 18: DOW After US Election

Technical Analyst

Being a technical analyst enables you to read the chart which allows you to get rid of fear, hope and greed. Have you ever seen charts when watching the news and wondered how you can make a decision or make money from the charts?

From the onset of my trading career, I was taught how to be a technical analyst by using several indicators such as stochastics, moving average (*Figure 19*) and reading the charts. A technical analyst trader learns how to develop his/her skill in the markets to learn how to read the charts to ensure they know where to buy or sell to maximise profits. A technical analyst trader has the benefit of not letting emotions get in the way. Their technique looks at price action, reading the charts and understanding human behaviour.

A skill every trader needs to develop is ability to identify market trends, ways to make money when market is going up or down and to buy at entry level or at beginning of a trend. As shown below (*Figure 20*), NAS100 moved over 2,737.10 points from the 2,887.9 entry level. Therefore, trading at £10 per points equates to £20,737.10 from 2013 – 2017 provided you are prepared to keep the trade open.

Figure 19: Trading Indicators, moving average

Figure 20: Trading Indicators, moving average

Once you have taken my trading programme, you will learn how to identify trends. The media will also let us know when a stock/FX market starts to sell we will lose money. A normal investor will question making money when the market goes down, this is possible as a trader. This sometimes baffles investors who have invested their money in the stock market for long term gain and then they may end up at the same level in 10 years' (*Figure 21*), not knowing that they have to improve their skills as an investor/trader to ensure they make money in an uptrend or a downtrend.

Figure 21: S&P 500 Stocks - 10 Year Period

News Trade

Trading the news can be very rewarding when you are on the right side of the market. Many clever traders would try to place a trade on either side and then get caught up in not being able to get out of the trade on time. Always have a trading plan as to where you will buy and where you are going to sell before the news. Simply so you don't get caught up in the heights of madness with emotion, as you see the market starting to move to the upside.

The spread is one important factor for a trader to bear in mind when they are trading as this determines your cost of doing business once you enter a trade. Trading the news will often cause some slippage and increase in spreads. The brokers' aim is to make money. Therefore, as many traders make most of their money during the news, the broker will increase the spread, as they too want to be a part of the party that makes money. The size of one's transaction has a part to play in the spread that a broker will give you. The larger your capital, the cheaper the spread.

Fundamental

The news is an essential part of trading and it drives the movement in the market. When there is a big announcement in the news about a particular country, this affects the different currencies. For example, when it was announced that the UK voted out of the European Union, the British Pound dropped in value on the FX market. Without news, FX would be absent of volume, making the market stagnant with very little movement (see example across). Another example would be before the ECB announcement on 5th June 2014, or any other countries major announcement, the price movements on the chart hardly moved: The Euro fell 1.3558, the lowest in four months. If you are a support and resistance trader you could trade this particular way. I will explain how you can benefit trading in this type of market as the market moves in three modes; uptrend, downtrend and sideways (consolidation). One of my trading strategies is to trade support and resistance when the market is trading sideways.

The market has gone through several crashes. For example, on the 19th of October 1987 described as Black Monday, many traders who placed an order, were not filled, prices were not updated, and brokers didn't answer their phones. This was one of those unusual crashes, as it was market-based and not an economic one.

Economic Data

Economic data has a great influence on the markets. The Us non-farm payrolls (employment figures) is very important data which is traded on most markets (*Figure 22*).

Figure 22: US Non-Farm Employment Change

During 1990 – 1991 there was an economic slowdown across the globe which included factors such as a slump in house prices, the first Gulf War and a rise in oil prices.

We are yet again going through another oil crisis, where the price of crude oil is below $40 per barrel, which means a lot of oil companies have gone bust. However, some traders make money in downturns.

Foreign Exchange Intervention

FX is where one currency is traded against another. The market sees market makers who thrive on trading on the excitement and anticipation of the news. From time to time, central banks from a different country will intervene. In 2015 the Bank of Japan intervened with its currency and we saw the market fall over 1,000 pips. I can remember this vividly, as I was providing an online mentoring session to my students, just as I advised them to trade GBP/JPY - the Great British Pound against the Japanese Yen, the market suddenly fell 1,000. Many of my students couldn't place an order to sell as brokers stopped traders from placing orders on the trading platform.

According to Sharpe (2012,) whenever particular rates exceed their parity band, an intervention is needed. In November 2015, the Euro was heading toward parity with the US Dollar. Here, an intervention by Draghi could have been useful.

The Swiss Franc is another example and very prone to having interventions by the central bank. During the recession, the government decided to weaken the Swiss Franc to combat deflationary pressures. knowing this information, one can increase their capital in anticipation of such an announcement (*Figure 23*).

Figure 23: EURCHF 4,000 pips move

CHAPTER 7

GROWTH

"I will tell you how to become rich. Close the doors. Be fearful when others are greedy. Be greedy when others are fearful."

Warren Buffett

Optimal Investment Anlyst Why do we invest?

Whether you invest in property or stocks/FX markets, you will gain ROI over time. From my experience while investing in property, I have been through ups and downs. Using the equity to create another property to add to my portfolio has helped me to understand the market and how you can repeat the same strategy if the return is reasonable.

Figure 24: Investor Diversification Growth

Having the right mindset and training, I started investing in property by attending a course called 'Women in Property.' This enabled me to have a better understanding of the market and how to make my money work for me by using the right tools and professionals on board to gain maximum profits.

The FX stocks or commodities markets are no different in regards to investing your money. Becoming an investor/trader will allow you to identify the best possible ways of making profits. With my programme, you will learn how to become an optimal investment analysis. Understanding how each market trades on a daily basis will keep you ahead of the trading game.

Having a portfolio that will allow you to trade all markets is important. Fund managers diversify their assets across all markets to alleviate losses. Why do some retail investors only own one stock or commodity? By portfolio diversification, this allows you to be able to withstand the market going up or down. For example, in commodities, crude oil has been trading below $50 per barrel for the last year, as a retail investor, having only crude oil in your portfolio, will wipe your account to zero. Therefore, the answer to ensure you stay afloat, is to become an investor/trader who diversifies the risk of his or her portfolio across all markets.

Growth

One of my personal development coaches is Tony Robbins and he talks about the six basic human needs. I would like to share them with you:

1. Growth
2. Contribute
3. Significance
4. Uncertainty
5. Certainty
6. Love & Connection

As this chapter is about growth, let's review the meaning of growth and how it can affect our lives on a daily/yearly basis. We have been taught to go to school, college, university and once we complete our education, we get a JoB (Just over Broke) and then wait for our retirement to creep up on us. Sadly, this model has resulted in many of our fore parents having to rely on the state and not take control of their own retirement or destiny.

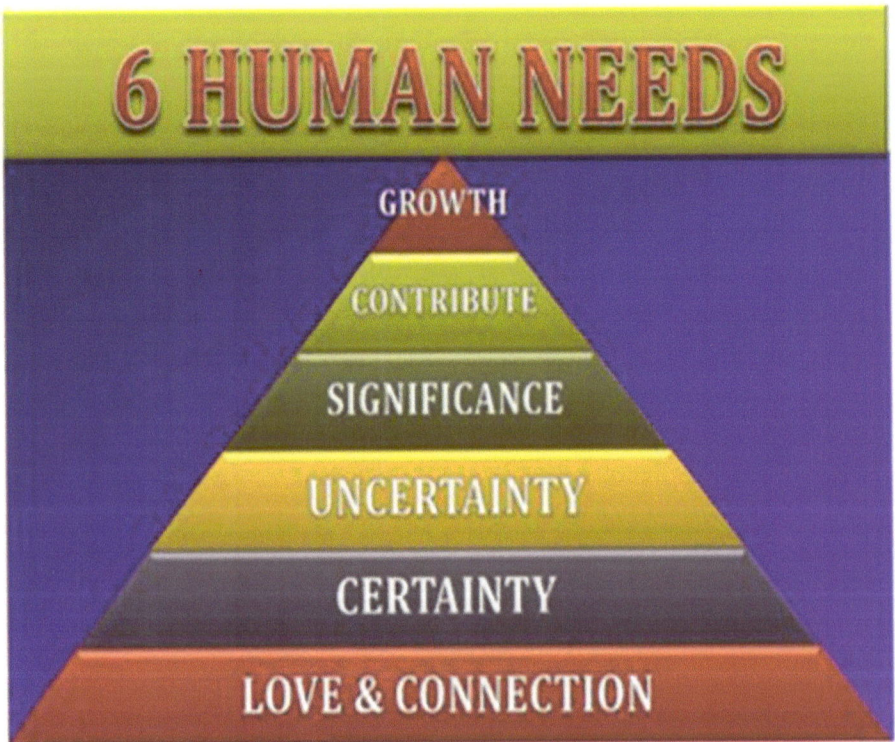

Figure 25: Tony Robbins – 6 Basic Human Needs

Have you ever wondered why most people stay in a mediocre career for so long? They are afraid of change. Investing in your financial, educational, emotional and spiritual growth will facilitate change and conquer fear of the unknown.

In previous chapters, I have discussed how you can acquire

growth and take control of your destiny by learning how to trade. My T.R.A.D.I.N.G. programme™ can allow you to build a future and leave a legacy for your children.

Often trading is described as a zero-sum game. in layman's terms, this means if one person is losing another is gaining.

"One man's loss is another man's gain"
Proverbs

There are various strategies in the market today about "growth and value investing." I will explain both and make comparisons relating to the market to ensure new and advanced investors/traders, can understand from each side, the benefits of aiming to increase your capital by growth.

The definition of 'growth investing' by Investopedia is as follows: "a strategy whereby an investor seeks out stocks with what they deem good growth potential. In most cases, a growth stock is defined as a company whose earnings are expected to grow at an above-average rate compared to its industry or the overall market."

Do you want to trade like a fund manager?

We can become our own fund manager by beating the banks and learning to become an investor/trader. A fund manager is one who will trade your money on your behalf to offer a good return.

There are differences between an investor and a trader.

Investor

An investor is often described as one who buys a stock, currency or commodity and holds on to it for a long period of time with the expectation that the price of what they have purchased, on behalf of their client, increases. Investors make money from buying. An investor will hold onto their stocks for a longer time frame, even when the price is going against them with the anticipation that one day it will exceed its original level of gains.

Trader

A trader is one who can read the charts to make the trading decision for percentage gain. A technical trader will trade the markets when it's going up or down to make money.

In 2009, when there was a market crash, many people lost money on the market because they were solely investors. As a trader you can make money by both buying and selling.

Earn extra

To generate consistent profits over the years as a short-term trader one can do so by consistently adding to your capital on a daily basis. This can be done by a percentage, earning extra each day. To transition from a part- time to a full-time trader, you should earn the same amount on your day job before taking on the role of a full-time trader. Many new traders give up their job before thinking of the costs involved in trading and there is a possibility that you may not be earning a reasonable income for the next six months or so until you develop the skills to become a proficient trader. Let's be real here, your bills still have to be paid. this is why the 95% of traders give up as they don't have sufficient money to fund their day- to -day living.

CHAPTER 8

BONUS

Trading for a Living (business)

Trading should be taken seriously, although it has a much smaller start-up cost than a franchise business. As a trader, you can earn a comfortable income to give up your day job. However, one has to be realistic about your capital investment as there are no guarantees. Firstly, educate yourself with the trading terminology, understand the market psychology, adopt discipline and develop risk management. Once you have mastered this, you can build a successful trading business.

80% of success is psychological and 20% is mechanism, the 80/20 rule or the Pareto Principle.

Best time to trade

I often get asked this question: "when is the best time to trade?" There is no best time to trade; I would tell my clients to be present and available in the market when you are trading.

Making sure you are aware of the economic calendar that can be found on www. forexfactory.com, which will give you a great advantage regarding trading times and news.

Short term position

A trader will hold a position for two days or a week in order to gain profits. This is often times called a swing trade. This type of trading is relevant for someone who has a busy lifestyle and does not have the time to sit in front a computer on a daily basis.

Long term position

This will allow a trader to leave his position on for more than a week, month or year. An investor will use this particular trading style to accumulate extreme profits, in particular, planning for retirement. The trade below shows (*Figure 26*) taking a long-term position as part of a retirement fund buying the FTSE 100 index (Uk100) from 3750.50 to 7327.8 since February 2003. As part of a retirement portfolio, investing in the FTSE fund would gain 3,576 points at £10 per contract, which equates to £35,760.

Figure 26: FTSE 100 Index

Be present with market events

With trading, you have to check the news calendar on a daily basis to ensure key events won't affect your trade. Be vigilant. This will also create opportunities on the chart to make money.

Market correlation

The Federal Reserve System which is the central banking system of the United States is due to raise interest rates. Therefore, the FX market is in anticipation that the dollar will increase (bearish).

Understanding this, a trader can then sell the British Pound against the Dollar. For example, the stock market such as S&P, DOW or NASDAQ will trade in the opposite direction meaning price would sell off against the dollar. Therefore, giving a trader the opportunity to make money knowing the market will go down (sell).

Trading journal

Trading should be treated as a business and not as a hobby. Traders' actions determine the success of their trades. Some will find every excuse as to why they can't review the markets. Others such as a shrewd businessman, would review his profit and loss, look at the actions he took, review when the best session is for his product and would ensure that he is always present or have adequate goods to support the peak times. Keep a record of all the transactions you make during your trading journal. You can then review this at the end of the week to see your best trading setup.

Develop a trading strategy

Before you enter the market, ensure you have a trading plan in place. Not having a trading plan will ruin your capital. You will need to know how you are going to enter (buy or sell), exit (take profit) and stop loss if the trade is going against you.

Major levels

There are levels that traders will remember. One of my trading strategies is to show you how to identify these levels so you have an advantage in the market and that you will make money trading these levels. (*Figure 27*).

Practice without risk

A broker will offer you the opportunity to practice before you start trading your money. This is often called a demo account. The good thing about demo accounts are that they allow you to practice a particular strategy to test if it works. Unlike a normal business,

Figure 27: Major level / Structural Failure CAD/JPY

where from the very beginning, you have to risk your real capital and learn from your mistakes.

Overtrading / emotional sabotage

Greed is one of the emotions that gets in the way of trading. Many traders will spend all day and night trading the markets. The initial attraction to trading for most is the possibility of decreasing working hours, but yet still some traders trade all day; winning and losing money because they cannot stop themselves from trading due to greed.

Social media

Companies will experience losses or lose business if they are not connected to their customers via social media. It is recorded that 90% of internet users are active on social media. 30% of time spent online is spent on Facebook. Fay & Thomas (2012) suggested that marketers have acknowledged the power of WoM (Word of Mouth) to shape the fortunes of their brands; however, they have done very little about it. Companies are now able to advertise on social media platforms such as Facebook, LinkedIn, Twitter, Instagram and Pinterest without spending huge amounts. Adverts placed on social media achieve incredible results at a fraction of the price when compared to traditional advertising mediums. Social media allows you to engage with your customers, in particular repeat customers who will stay with you much longer (Faye & Thomas, 2012).

The growing rate of social media is far beyond our comprehension. The use of Facebook has increased enormously. The use of social media is critical for any business and it has a vital role to play in how companies advertise their product or services. Using LinkedIn, Twitter, Instagram and Facebook are the main avenues to promote products. Companies use these websites/apps to advertise products as a cheaper method. Getting consumers to like a product and share within their network will increase brand awareness of that particular product or service. Getting customers to write and recommend a product is a way of increasing sales. This is a brilliant form of WoM of buying decision (Euromonitor, 2012).

Connect with me on Social media!

@janetfxblair - @tradesmarterfx - @thejanetblair - JanetBlairmba,msc

QUESTIONS

ARE YOU READY TO GAIN MORE KNOWLEDGE?

There are several questions you may be asking yourself. But let me try and answer some of these questions for you.

Q: *Do I need a degree to become a trader?*
A: No, absolutely not. No formal qualifications required.

Q: *I do not have the expert knowledge, can I still trade?*
A: You will develop knowledge and become an expert by taking my T.R.A.D.I.N.G. Programme™. www.thejanetblair.com

Q: *Will I lose money?*
A: Trading is a business of risk, but with good risk management in place, you can minimise losses.

Q: *Isn't it bad to trade, as the media says it's risky?*
A: The media will scare you, if you continue to listen. In fact, the Media generally has negative things to say about most things in life. Managing your risk is important and this you will learn on my T.R.A.D.I.N.G. programme™.

Q: *I can't seem to find the 'Holy Grail,' is there one for trading?*
A: There is no such thing as the 'holy grail' for traders, find a system that you are comfortable with and practice.

Q: *I have advanced knowledge about the markets but I can't seem to*

make any money. Where am I going wrong?
A: Many traders go through this as they do not have a coach/mentor to guide them. Getting a coach/mentor will enhance your trading journey to become a consistent trader.

Q: *Where should I buy or sell?*
A: A very good question which has frequently been asked. This book will show you how and where to buy or sell to make a profit.

Q: *Where should I place my stop?*
A: Stop loss is paramount to your trading success; this book is written with you in mind to show you the exact level of where to place your stop.

Q: *What mindset do I need to become a trader?*
A: To become a successful trader, you have to develop the right mindset, which is discussed in this book.

Q: *Where can I research online and gain extensive knowledge?*
A: There are several online courses and scammers and it's best to learn from someone who you can connect with directly, not just an online system.

Q: *Can I practice using a demo account?*
a: You can practice with a demo account to gain more confidence and learn different FX trading strategies.

Q: *Do you suggest any particular brokers?*
A: *I will discuss how yo*u can choose a broker in this book.

Q: *Do I need a trading mentor/coach?*
A: If you want to become successful you will need a coach/mentor. Just as a footballer or a tennis player has a coach to succeed.

Q: *How long will it take me to learn?*
A: Trading the markets is very simple with my programme. However, everyone learns differently so it's entirely up to you how many hours you put into the markets to learn initially.

Q: *Is it for women as well as men?*
A: FX, stocks, commodities and equities markets are for everyone. It doesn't matter whether you are male or female.

Q: *I don't have much spare time; can I still learn?*
A: With trading the markets, you don't need a lot of time, you can be in the markets for 30 minutes or 4 hours.

Q: *How do I manage my money?*
A: Money management is the key to preserving your trading capital; this will be discussed in this book.

Q: *I don't have enough to start trading?*
A: Trading is one of the lowest capital start-up businesses you can get into. You don't need a lot of money to start your trading fund.

Q: *My friends and family say I am gambling, is that what FX is?*
A: Friends and family who have this opinion, don't understand the concept of trading. Trading is a business. Find people who are traders to be around and to help you to remain focused.

THANK YOU

Well done for reading this book to the end and taking the time out to cover how the Foreign exchange (FX) market works. As a thank you for completing my book, I have included a list of bonuses for you, which I have found useful over the years.

Access to 5 Secrets to Double Your Trading Account in 30 Days, Thanks to Forex:
http://www.thejanetblair.com/Webinar

Private 30 minute 1-on-1 session when you purchase my 3 Day Trading Workshop.
Trading blogs:
http://www.thejanetblair.com/trading-blog/

Trade Smarter FX Trading Journal:
http://www.thejanetblair.com/Journal

I really appreciate your time in reading The Trading Floor and understanding the materials illustrated in this book. Look no further, you have made the right decision to learn to trade FX as this offers many advantages.

For further learning of trading strategies and techniques you can visit http://www.thejanetblair.com/90 or you can contact me at janet@ thejanetblair.com.

GOOD LUCK ON YOUR TRADING JOURNEY!

REFERENCES

https://www.brainyquote.com/quotes/quotes/w/winston-chu104164.html http://www.brainyquote.com/quotes/quotes/c/charlescal386336.html

Doyle, P. (2008) Value-based marketing: marketing strategies for corporate growth and shareholder value. 2nd Ed. England: John Wiley & Son, Ltd

https://www.fool.com/investing/general/2014/09/28/25-best-warren-buffett-quotes....

https://www.goodreads.com/quotes/219455-the-secret-of-getting-ahead-is-getting-s... http://www.harveker.com/secretsofthemillionairemind http://www.investopedia.com/terms/forex/f/foreign-exchange-markets.asp

Key note (2013) Financial services organisations on the internet market assessment 2013 (online) available from: http://www.keynote.co.uk.lispac.lsbu.ac.uk// financial-services-organisa-tions-on-the-internet?highlight=word+of+mouth+- mobile+tech-nology&utm_source=kn.reports.search

https://quizlet.com/227661/investopedia-flash-cards/

Ritholtz, B., (2009) Bailout nation; how greed and easy money corrupted Wall street and shoot the world economy, John Wiley & Sons, Inc., Hoboken, New Jersey

Sharpe, James (2012) Foreign exchange: the complete deal, a comprehensive guide to the theory and practise of the FX market Harriman House Ltd, Hampshire Great Britain

https://www.stocktrader.com/2009/05/14/
trading-psychology-stages-investor-emotio…

https://www.tonyrobbins.com/

GLOSSARY

Abbreviation

Major Currency Pairs
Euro (EUR)
Japanese Yen (JPY)
Pound sterling (GBP)
Swiss Franc (CHF)
US Dollar (USD)

Commodities Currencies:
Australia (AUD)
Canada (CAD)
New Zealand (NZD)
Norway (NOR)
South Africa (ZAR)

Definitions

Analyst
An expert who analyses the markets to identify which currency to buy or sell before the trading session.

Asian session
23:00 - 08:00 GMT.

Ask (offer) price
The price at which the market is prepared to sell a product. Price can be quoted in two ways, the Bid/Ask. This price is also known as the offer.

Aussie
This refers to the Australian dollar against the Us dollar (ASD/USD)

Base currency
This refers to the first currency in the pair. eg: USD/JPY - US dollar being the base currency in this instance.

Bear/bearish market
Price declines to the downside. When the market is weak and you have more sellers than buyers in the market.

Bid/ask spread
The difference between the bid and the asking price.

BOC
The Canadian central bank, Bank of Canada.

BOE
The UK central bank, Bank of England.

BOJ
The Japanese central bank, Bank of Japan.

Broker
This could be an individual or company who connects the buyer and the seller for a fee or commission.

Bull/bullish market
When price rises to the upside. The market will be classed as strong because prices are trading much higher.

Buy
Executing a long position on an instrument eg: EUR/USD

Candlestick chart
This shows where the price opens and closes for the day. If price opens higher than it closes, the candle will be shaded.

Capitulation
During an extreme trend, traders who are losing will often exit from their position. It's the expectation that the market will reverse soon.

Chart
This shows price action over a particular timeframe (5min, 30min, one hour, monthly or yearly). This may either be a bar/candlesticks chart.

Closing
To stop a live trade position that has been executed in the opposite position.

Commission
The broker will charge a fee for the buying and selling position which is often called the spread.

Contract
A standard unit of trading.

Cross
Any other currency excluding the US Dollar.

Currency
Money issued by the government or central bank that is used as legal tender to purchase goods or services in a particular area.

*Curren***cy pairs**
Two currencies that traded in the FX market, eg: GBP/USD.

Daily chart
This displays the daily movements of a currency pair.

Day trader
A speculator who take positions in the FX market and then closed these position before the end of day.

Dealing Desk
This is the platform for dealing with issues to do with pricing of shares as well as facilitating a smooth exchange of both currency pairs and information relating to FX. Sometimes a broker may choose to forego the need for the dealing desk. The role of these people is left in the hands of the liquidity providers who are sourced from the outside of the FX market.

Deficit
A negative balance of trade or payments.

Downtrend
A series of lower low and lower highs.

ECB
Countries using the Euro undertake transaction with the European Central Bank.

Economic indicator
This reflects the health of an economy and is responsible for the shift in supply and demand.

Economic of sales
Savings that can be achieved through increased size.

Entry
A transaction that happens when the trader decides to either buy or sell a currency pair.

Euro
The currency of the Eurozone.

European session
07:00 - 16:00 (London).

Exchange Rate
The exchange rate of one currency is measured by that of another country. This is where currency pairs come from. Currency pairs result from the pairing of currencies for the purpose of determining the exchange rate and by extension, facilitating the calculation of profits to be realised by FX traders. When one currency has been sold; it goes without saying that the other one has been bought.

Exit
When a trader decides to close their position for either profit or loss.

FED
The central bank of the United States, or the FoMc (Federal open

Market committee), the Federal Reserve Bank; a policy setting committee of the Federal Reserve.

Fill
An order that is fully executed.

Foreign Exchange (Forex, FX)
This is a large market where the business of exchanging currencies at a profit is carried out. There is no meeting place, and therefore it is not a market in the conventional sense. Most of the deals are negotiated through the network consisting of individual investors, brokerage firms as well as FX trade companies. FX is the largest tradeable market in the world which is unregulated. On a daily basis, transactions amount to over $5 Trillion. The market is open 24 hours per day, five days a week.

FTSE 100 Index
The Financial Times stock exchange 100 index, 100 UK largest top quality companies.

Initial margin
The initial amount you place a trade to either buy or sell.

Interbank
This refers to a network consisting of investment banks, big corporations, insurance and reinsurance companies. This network serves to manage risks that arise as a result of fluctuating exchange rates.

Interest rate
A lender or borrower may charge a particular amount which is expressed in a percentage format. The federal bank will increase or decrease interest rates based on the financial stability of a country. This will then be passed on to retailers that will make changes to mortgages, loans, and price of goods/services.

Limit order
An order placed by a customer to buy or sell a currency or stock.

Liquidity
The acceptance of a large transaction that has a minimal impact on price stability.

Long position
This means, when a trader thinks the market will rise, he/she believes the price will go up. as the trader would say, 'I am in a long (buy) position.'

Margin
A margin is a required amount that a trader must deposit to enter a position (buy or sell). A fee margin means the entire amount which is available for any trader to execute a trade to buy or sell.

Margin call
A request from the broker for additional funds, if the buy or sell position a trader takes moves in the opposite direction.

Market makers
A market maker is a pricing specialist who traces the progress of a single currency pair. It indicates the readiness of the market to accept the buying and selling prices. The market maker however, has the authority of off-setting the imbalances that exist in the trade as well as manage them. This ensures stability in the whole of the forex trade. The commission that the market marker earns arises from the difference between the offer value and the bid value. A market maker provides a place for bankers to place their bids. Since these bids are often conflicting in most cases each party to the transaction feels compelled to push for the most reasonable deal.

Market order
An order that is placed in the market to execute immediately at current market price. This order is filled as long as there are buyers and sellers in the market. This is a type of order.

PIP
The measurement of price as to how far a currency pair price has moved eg: If you bought the GBP/USD at 1.3030 and it rose to 1.3050, it means you have gained 20 pips.

Position
The total amount of a currency to keep a trader in the trade.

Profit target
An area on the chart where you believe price will reach in order to gain profit. Before you enter a trade, if all goes well and your target is reached you will make profit on the trade you have taken.

Quote
The is normally used for information purposes as an indication of the market price.

Risk
The amount a trader is prepared to lose in one or several trades they have placed an order to either buy or sell.

Sell quote/buy quote
Sell quote is the price at which currency is sold. It is the price which is displayed as the bid and it is shown on the left of the transaction board. The buy quote is shown on the right. This is the buying price of the currency.

Short sell
An investor/trader, borrows money from the broker by selling them with the intention of buying them in the future.

Spot market
This is the market where one can buy and sell currencies of different countries at the prevailing exchange rate.

Spread
A broker is paid by commission which is called the spread. The difference between the bid (buy) and ask (sell) price, for example the Bid EUR/USD 1.2220 and Ask 1.2225. This means the broker would earn five pips spread and this is described as a trader's cost.

Stop loss order
An order placed with a broker to minimise a trader's losses. This is placed on a trader's trading platform in a buy or sell position, when price reaches a particular level the trade will be closed.

Trading Platform
This is used by traders to place an order to buy or sell, much like a command centre. You inform the broker of your intentions before you execute your trade.

Volatility
Over a given time frame a measurement in price change in the currency market.

Whipsaw
A very volatile market condition that is often used by traders, in particular around news events. The price will increase or decrease sharply within seconds.